Merry Christmas with Love

A Celebration of Christmas Traditions

Copyright © 1994

Brownlow Publishing Company

6309 Airport Freeway

Fort Worth, Texas 76117

ISBN 1-57051-022-9

Cover/interior:

Koechel Peterson & Associates

Printed in USA

A Special Gift

FOR:

Dolores

FROM:

Ronda

DATE:

12/25/99

Merry Christmas with Love

Brownlow

Edited by Paul C. Brownlow

A Christmas Song

Oh, Christmas is a jolly time
When forests hang with snow,
And other forests bend with toys,
And lordly Yule logs glow.

And Christmas is a solemn time
Because, beneath the star,
The first great
Christmas Gift was given
To all men, near and far.

But not alone at Christmas time
Comes holiday and cheer,
For one who loves a little child
Hath Christmas all the year.

FLORENCE EVELYN DRATT

Ye Who Have Loved

Ye who have loved each other,
Sister and friend and brother,
In this fast fading year;
Mother and sire and child,
Young man and maiden mild,
Come gather here.

Let sinned against, and sinning
Forget their strife's beginning,
And join in friendship now:
Be links no longer broken,
Be sweet forgiveness spoken,
Under the Holly bough.

CHARLES MACKAY

Home for Christmas

This is meeting time again. Home is the magnet. The winter land roars and hums with the eager speed of return journeys. The dark is noisy and bright with late-night arrivals—doors thrown open, running shadows on snow, open arms, kisses, voices and laughter, laughter at everything and nothing. Inarticulate, giddying and confused are those original minutes of being back again. The very familiarity of everything acts like shock. Contentment has to be drawn in slowly, steadyingly, in deep breaths—there is so much of it. We rely on home not to change, and it does not, wherefore we give thanks. Again Christmas: abiding point of return. Set apart by its mystery, mood and magic, the season seems in a way to stand outside time. All that is dear, that is lasting, renews its hold on us; we are home again.

This glow of Christmas, has it not in it also the gold of a harvest? *They shall return with joy, bringing their sheaves with them.* To the festival, to each other, we

bring in wealth. More to tell, more to understand, more to share. Each we have garnered in yet another year; to be glad, to celebrate to the full, we are come together. How akin we are to each other, how speechlessly dear and one in the fundamentals of being, Christmas shows us. No other time grants us, quite, this vision—round the tree or gathered before the fire we perceive anew, with joy, one another's faces. And each time faces come to mean more.

Is it not one of the mysteries of life that life should, after all, be so simple? Yes, as simple as Christmas, simple as this. Journeys through the dark to lighted door, arms open. Laughter-smothered kisses, kiss-smothered laughter. And blessedness in the heart of it all. Dearer than memory, brighter than expectation is the ever returning *now* of Christmas. Why else, each time we greet its return, should happiness ring out in us like a peal of bells?

ELIZABETH BOWEN

Lady Caroline's Peppermint Snaps

INGREDIENTS

Cookies

1 cup shortening
1 cup firmly packed brown sugar
1 egg
$1^1/_2$ cups flour
$^1/_2$ teaspoon baking soda
$^1/_2$ teaspoon salt
$1^1/_2$ cups quick or old-fashioned oats,
uncooked
$^1/_2$ cup crushed peppermint candy

Glaze

1 cup powdered sugar
2 to 3 tablespoons milk
$^1/_2$ teaspoon peppermint extract
1 drop red food coloring

COOKING INSTRUCTIONS

Cookies

- Beat together shortening and sugar until light and fluffy.
- Blend in egg. Add combined dry ingredients; mix well.
- Stir in oats and peppermint candy.
- Shape dough to form 1½-inch balls.
- Place about 2 inches apart on ungreased cookie sheet; flatten with tines of fork.
- Bake in preheated 375°F oven 8 to 10 minutes or until golden brown.
- Cool 1 minute before removing from cookie sheet.

Glaze

- Combine all ingredients; mix well.
- Drizzle over cooled cookies.

Makes about 2½ dozen cookies.

Incarnate Love

Love came down at Christmas,
Love all lovely, Love Divine;
Love was born at Christmas,
Star and angels gave the sign.

Love shall be our token,
Love be yours and Love be mine,
Love to God and all men,
Love for plea and gift and sign.

CHRISTINA ROSSETTI

Merry Christmas Morning

A Merry Christmas morning
To each and every one!
The rose has kissed the dawning
And the gold is in the sun.

And may the Christmas splendor
A joyous greeting bear,
Of love that's true and tender
And faith that's sweet and fair!

Song of Christmas

Sing a song of Christmas!
Pockets full of gold;
Plums and cakes
for Polly's stocking,
More than it can hold.
Pudding in the great pot,
Turkey on the spit,
Merry faces round the fire,—
Smiling quite a bit!

Sing a song of Christmas!
Carols in the street,
People going home with bundles
Everywhere we meet.
Holly, fir, and spruce boughs
Green upon the wall,
Spotless snow upon the road,—
More about to fall.

UNKNOWN

IT CAME UPON THE MIDNIGHT CLEAR

It came upon the midnight clear,
That glorious song of old,
From angels bending near the earth,
To touch their harps of gold:
"Peace on the earth, good-will to men,
From heaven's all gracious King":
The world in solemn stillness lay
To hear the angels sing.

Still through the cloven skies they come,
With peaceful wings unfurled;
And still their heavenly music floats
O'er all the weary world:
Above its sad and lowly plains
They bend on hovering wing,
And ever o'er its Babel sounds
The blessed angels sing.

EDMUND H. SEARS

Christmas Bells

Hark! the Christmas bells are ringing—
　Ringing through the frosty air—
　Happiness to each one bringing,
　And release from toil and care.

How the merry peal is swelling
From the gray old crumbling tower,
　To the simplest creature telling
　Of Almighty love and power.

Ankle-deep the snow is lying,
　Every spray is clothed in white,
　Yet abroad the folk are hieing,
　Brisk and busy, gay and light.

Now fresh helps and aids are offered
　To the aged and the poor;
　And rare love-exchanges proffered
　At the lowliest cottage door.

Neighbors shaking hands and greeting,
　No one sorrowing, no one sad,
　Children, loving parents meeting,
　Young and old alike are glad.

Then while Christmas bells are ringing,
　Rich and poor, your voices raise,
　And—your simple carol singing—
　Waft to heaven your grateful praise.

UNKNOWN

Childlike Faith

Whatever else be lost among the years,
Let us keep Christmas still a shining thing:
Whatever doubts assail us, or what fears,
Let us hold close one day, remembering
Its poignant meaning for the hearts of men.
Let us get back our childlike faith again.

GRACE NOLL CROWELL

The Spirit of Giving

When the Child of Nazareth was born, the sun, according to the Bosnian legend, "leaped in the heavens, and the stars around it danced. A peace came over mountain and forest. Even the rotten stump stood straight and healthy on the green hill-side. The grass was beflowered with open blossoms, incense sweet as myrrh pervaded upland and forest, birds sang on the mountain top, and all gave thanks to the great God."

It is naught but an old folk-tale, but it has truth hidden at its heart, for a strange, subtle force, a spirit of genial good-will, a new-born kindness, seem to animate child and man alike when the world pays its tribute to the "heaven-sent youngling," as the poet Drummond calls the infant Christ.

When the Three Wise Men rode from the East into the West on that "first, best Christmas night," they bore on their saddlebows three caskets filled with gold and frankincense and myrrh, to be laid at the feet of the manger-cradled Babe of Bethlehem. Beginning with this old, old journey, the spirit of giving crept into the world's heart. As the Magi came bearing gifts, so do we also—gifts that relieve wants, gifts that are sweet and fragrant with friendship, gifts that breathe love, gifts that mean service, gifts inspired still by the star that shone over the City of David nearly two thousand years ago.

Then hang the green coronet of the Christmas-tree with glittering baubles and jewels of flame; heap offerings on its emerald branches; bring the Yule log to the firing; deck the house with holly and mistletoe,

"And all the bells on
  earth shall ring
On Christmas day
  in the morning."

KATE DOUGLAS WIGGIN

If I Knew

If I knew where to find him,
The baby in the hay,
I'd take a Christmas present
To him this very day:
Two little hands to serve him,
And a loving heart to lift,
And just myself on Christmas day
To be his birthday gift.

UNKNOWN

A Christmas Tree

I have been looking on, this evening, at a merry company of children assembled round that pretty German toy, a Christmas Tree. The tree was planted in the middle of a great round table, and towered high above their heads. It was brilliantly lighted by a multitude of little tapers; and everywhere sparkled and glittered with bright objects. There were rosy-cheeked dolls, hiding behind the green leaves; and there were real watches (with movable hands, at least, and an endless capacity of being wound up) dangling from innumerable twigs; there were French-polished tables, chairs, bedsteads, wardrobes, eight-day clocks, and various other articles of domestic furniture (wonderfully made, in tin, at Wolverhampton), perched among the boughs; there were jolly, broad-faced little men, much more agreeable in appearance than many real men—and no wonder, for their heads took off, and showed them to be full of sugar-plums; there were fiddles and drums; there were tambourines, books, work-boxes, paint boxes, sweetmeat boxes, peep-show boxes, and all kinds of boxes; there were trinkets for the elder girls, far brighter than any grown-up gold and jewels; there were baskets and pincushions in all devices; there were guns, swords, and banners; there were teetotums, humming-tops, needle-cases, pen-wipers, smelling-bottles, conversation-cards, bouquet-holders; real fruit, made artificially dazzling with gold leaf; imitation apples, pears, and walnuts, crammed with surprises; in short, as a pretty child, before me, delightedly whispered to another pretty child, her bosom friend, "There was everything, and more."

CHARLES DICKENS

Christmas Gifts

The wondrous love and light,
The fullness and the glory,
The meaning and the might,
Of all the Christmas story,
May Christ Himself
unfold to you today,
And bid you go rejoicing
on your way.

A happy, happy Christmas,
Be yours today!
Oh, not the failing measure
Of fleeting earthly pleasure,
But Christmas joy abiding,
While years are swiftly gliding,
Be yours, I pray,
Through Him who
gave us Christmas-day!

A bright and blessed
Christmas-day,

With echoes of the angels' song,
And peace that
cannot pass away,
And holy gladness,
calm and strong,
And sweet heart carols,
flowing free!
This is my Christmas
wish to thee!

Down the ages hoary
Peals the song of glory,
Peace, and God's good-will!
Other echoes die away,
But the song of Christmas-day
Echoes from the Judean hill,
Ever clearer, louder still.
Oh, may its holy, heavenly chime
Make all thy life
a Christmas-time!

FRANCES RIDLEY HAVERGAL

Christmas Cake (Fruitcake)

INGREDIENTS

3 cups all-purpose flour

2 teaspoons baking powder

1 teaspoon salt

1 tablespoon ground cinnamon

1 teaspoon ground nutmeg

$^1/_2$ teaspoon ground allspice

2 cups chopped mixed candied fruits

2 cups raisins

1 cup golden raisins

$1^1/_4$ cups chopped pitted dates

2 cups coarsely chopped walnuts

4 eggs

2 cups packed dark brown sugar

$1^1/_4$ cups orange juice

$^3/_4$ cup ($1^1/_2$ sticks) butter,
melted and cooled

$^1/_4$ cup molasses

COOKING INSTRUCTIONS

Preheat the oven to 300°F. Grease two 9-inch-by-5-inch loaf pans and line them with waxed paper.

- Whisk together the flour, baking powder, salt, and spices. Add the candied fruits, raisins, dates, and nuts, and toss to coat them with the dry ingredients.

- Beat the eggs with an electric mixer until light. Mix in the brown sugar, orange juice, melted butter, and molasses. Add this to the fruit mixture and stir well. Spoon the batter into the prepared pans to fill about halfway.

- Bake for 2 hours or until a toothpick inserted in the centers comes out clean. Let the cakes cool in their pans set on wire racks.

- When they're cool, turn out the cakes from the pans and peel off the waxed paper. Wrap them in foil or plastic to keep moist and refrigerate until serving. They keep for up to a month.

More to Christmas

There's more, much more, to Christmas
Than candlelight and cheer;
It's the spirit of sweet friendship,
That brightens all the year;
It's thoughtfulness and kindness,
It's hope reborn again,
For peace, for understanding
And for goodwill to men!

ANONYMOUS

Christmas Tonight!

Everywhere, everywhere,
Christmas tonight!
Christmas in lands of the palm tree and vine;
Christmas where snow-peaks stand solemn and white,
Christmas where cornfields lie sunny and bright.

PHILLIPS BROOKS

Christmas

The earth has grown old with its burden of care
But at Christmas it always is young,
The heart of the jewel burns lustrous and fair
And its soul full of music breaks forth on the air,
When the song of the angels is sung.

The feet of the humblest may walk in the field
Where the feet of the holiest have trod,
This, this is the marvel to mortals revealed
When the silvery trumpets of Christmas have pealed,
That mankind are children of God.

PHILLIPS BROOKS

Christmas in the Heart

It is Christmas in the mansion,
Yule-log fires and silken frocks;
It is Christmas in the cottage,
Mother's filling little socks.

It is Christmas on the highway,
In the thronging, busy mart;
But the dearest, truest Christmas
Is the Christmas in the heart.

UNKNOWN

Christmas the Whole Year Through

*W*ho can be insensible to the outpourings of good feeling, and the honest interchange of affectionate attachment which abound at this season of the year. A Christmas family-party! We know nothing in nature more delightful! There seems a magic in the very name of Christmas. Petty jealousies and discords are forgotten; social feelings are awakened, in bosoms to which they have long been strangers; father and son, or brother and

sister, who have met and passed with averted gaze, or a look of cold recognition, for months before, proffer and return the cordial embrace, and bury their past animosities in their present happiness. Kindly hearts that have yearned towards each other but have been withheld by false notions of pride and self-dignity, are again reunited, and all is kindness and benevolence! Would that Christmas lasted the whole year through (as it ought) and that the prejudices and passions which deform our better nature were never called into action among those to whom they should ever be strangers!

CHARLES DICKENS

Almond Tea Punch

INGREDIENTS

1/2 cup lemon juice
2 cups sugar
1 cup strong tea
1 tablespoon vanilla flavoring
2 tablespoons almond flavoring
1 quart water
2-liter bottle ginger ale

INSTRUCTIONS

- Make a base of the following: 1/2 cup lemon juice, 2 cups sugar, 1 cup strong tea, 1 tablespoon vanilla flavoring, 2 tablespoons almond flavoring, 1 quart water.

- Freeze the base in a heavy-duty zip-lock bag.

- One hour before serving, take bag out of freezer. Put frozen base in punch bowl. Gently break it apart with a large fork.

- Add one 2-liter bottle of cold ginger ale to 1 part base.

Merry Christmas

In the rush of the merry morning,
When the red burns through the gray,
And the wintry world lies waiting
For the glory of the day;
Then we hear a fitful rushing
Just without upon the stair,
See three white phantoms coming,
Catch the gleam of sunny hair.

Rosy feet upon the threshold,
Eager faces peeping through,
With the first red ray of sunshine,
Chanting cherubs come in view;
Mistletoe and gleaming holly,
Symbols of a blessed day,
In their chubby hands they carry,
Streaming all along the way.

Well we know them, never weary
Of their innocent surprise:
Waiting, watching, listening always
With full hearts and tender eyes,
While our little household angels,
White and golden in the sun,
Greet us with the sweet old welcome,—
"Merry Christmas, every one!"

UNKNOWN

ROSES MAY COME
AND ROSES MAY GO

BUT CHRISTMAS BRINGS
THE MISTLETOE.

A Christmas Greeting

Dead are the asters by the roadside drear;
The days are short, the winter's snows are here:
Beside the Christmas hearth my thoughts still stray
To memories of the summer passed away.

When, wandering along some rocky shore,
We heard each other's thoughts, as ne'er before;
Or, sailing o'er the ocean, sparkling blue,
We saw old scenes with eyes that made them new.

When, stretched at length on some soft grassy bed,
We heard the birds sing in the boughs o'er head;
And, when the blood-red sun was dropping low,
Through the salt meadows took our evening row.

Gone are the days of summer, long and fair,
Dark are the evenings now, and chill the air,
As from my fireside unto thine I send
A Christmas greeting from a summer's friend.

UNKNOWN

Somehow not only

for Christmas

but all the long

year through,

the joy that

you give others

is the joy that

comes back to you.

JOHN GREENLEAF WHITTIER

I love the

Christmas-tide,

and yet I notice this,

each year I live;

I always like

the gifts I get,

But how I love

the gifts I give!

CAROLYN WELLS

Aunt LaVerne's Float (Eggnog)

INGREDIENTS

6 eggs*
1¼ cup sugar
2½ heaping tablespoons of cornstarch
1 large can of evaporated milk
½ gallon of whole milk
2 teaspoons vanilla

INSTRUCTIONS

Mix 6 egg yolks,* 1¼ cup sugar and
2½ heaping tablespoons of cornstarch in a
large, heavy saucepan. Add 1 large can of
evaporated milk. Stir together. Add ½ gallon
of whole milk. Stir constantly over low
heat until thick. Meanwhile, beat 6 egg
whites. Fold egg whites into custard and
then beat with electric mixer until fluffy.
Add 2 teaspoons vanilla.

Pour into large container. Sprinkle nutmeg
on top. Chill in refrigerator. Serve.

*Egg substitute may be used for egg yolks.

O holy Infant, small and dear,

Your birthday once again is here,

And joyful songs ring near and far

Wherever little children are.

O LITTLE TOWN OF BETHLEHEM

O little town of Bethlehem,
How still we see thee lie!
Above thy deep and dreamless sleep
The silent stars go by;
Yet in thy dark streets shineth
The everlasting Light;
The hopes and fears of all the years
Are met in thee to-night.

For Christ is born of Mary,
And, gathered all above,
While mortals sleep, the angels keep
Their watch of wondering love.
O morning stars, together
Proclaim the holy birth!
And praises sing to God the King,
And peace to men on earth.

PHILLIPS BROOKS

My Christmas-Day

There is a Christmas-time I knew
Within the long ago,
O'er which the fleeting years have passed,
And drifted deep their snow.

All fresh it lies, within my heart,
A spot of living green,
Undimmed by sorrow's bitter tide,
Or strifes that come between.

Like violet buds, enwreathed in green,
When snow-drifts melt away,
The joyous memories buried there
Lift up their heads, today.

And like the fragrance, purple dyed,
That breathes above the place,
So haloes all those far-off days
My mother's tender face.

O patient heart and busy hand,
How small the rest they know,
Within that palace of my heart,
The home of long ago!

O anxious, widowed, mother heart,
With double weight to bear,
How little did your children know
Of want, or strife, or care!

What triumph more sublime than yours
Above the arts of fate?
What hero's nobler fame is scrolled
In letters, war, or state?

Can I forget those stockings, filled
From top to bulging toe
By mother hands, at Christmas-time,
Within the long ago?

The little mittens, apple red,
Of yarn she spun and dyed,
The dollies cut from sweetened dough,
With spice-filled eyes, and fried.

With nuts and goodies, packed in close,
And maple sugar, run
In moulds with scalloped edges, laid
To top out every one.

Dear, struggling, anxious, patient heart,
Oh would that I, as then,
Might look into your loving eyes
And greet you once again!

For only years can teach the child
A mother's love to know;
And could I catch your listening ear,
I straight would tell you so.

And you, with old-time tender smile,
Forgetting self, would say:
"Run quickly, dear, the children call,
This is their Christmas-day."

HELEN D'AUBRY DURAND

God Bless Us Every One

Hallo! A great deal of steam! The pudding was out of the copper. A smell like a washing-day! That was the cloth. A smell like an eating-house and a pastrycook's next door to each other, with a laundress's next door to that! That was the pudding! In half a minute Mrs. Cratchit entered—flushed, but smiling proudly—with the pudding, like a speckled cannon-ball, so hard and firm, and bedight with Christmas holly stuck into the top.

Oh, what a wonderful pudding! Bob Cratchit said, and calmly too, that he regarded it as the greatest success achieved by Mrs. Cratchit since their marriage. Mrs. Cratchit said that now the weight was off her mind, she would confess she had had her doubts about the quantity of flour. Everybody had something to say about it, but nobody said or thought it was at all a small pudding for a large family. It would have been flat heresy to do so. Any Cratchit would have blushed to hint at such a thing.

At last the dinner was all done, the cloth was cleared, the hearth swept, and the fire made up. The compound in the jug being tasted, and considered perfect, apples and oranges were put upon the table, and a shovel-full of chestnuts on the fire. Then all the Cratchit family drew round the hearth, in what Bob Cratchit called a circle, meaning half a one; and at Bob Cratchit's elbow stood the family display of glass. Two tumblers, and a custard-cup without a handle.

These held the hot stuff from the jug, however, as well as golden goblets would have done; and Bob served it out with beaming looks, while the chestnuts on the fire sputtered and cracked noisily. Then Bob proposed:

"A Merry Christmas to us all, my dears. God bless us!"

Which all the family re-echoed.

"God bless us every one!" said Tiny Tim, the last of all.

A CHRISTMAS CAROL BY CHARLES DICKENS

Victorian
Plum Pudding

INGREDIENTS

Pudding

10 slices white bread
1 cup scalded milk
$^1/_2$ cup sugar
4 eggs, separated
1$^1/_3$ cups golden raisins, lightly floured
$^1/_2$ cup finely chopped dates
3 tablespoons finely chopped citron
$^3/_4$ cup finely chopped suet
1 teaspoon nutmeg
$^1/_2$ teaspoon cinnamon
$^1/_4$ teaspoon ground cloves
$^1/_4$ teaspoon mace
1 teaspoon salt

Hard Sauce

5 tablespoons butter
1 cup confectioners' sugar
$^1/_2$ teaspoon vanilla

COOKING INSTRUCTIONS

Pudding

- Crumb bread and soak in hot milk. Cool and add sugar, egg yolks, raisins, dates, and citron.
- Cream suet in food processor and add to crumb mixture. Stir in nutmeg, cinnamon, cloves, mace, and salt. Beat until well blended.
- Beat egg whites until stiff but not dry. Stir a third of the egg whites into pudding mixture; gently fold in the remainder.
- Spoon mixture into a buttered 2-quart mold and cover.
- Steam for 6 hours in a large covered pot holding boiling water to come halfway up the sides of the mold.

- Remove and let cool for 10 minutes before unmolding.
- Serve with warm hard sauce.

Hard Sauce

- Cream butter, add sugar; beat with electric beater until pale and creamy.
- Add vanilla and blend.
- Cover and refrigerate until needed.

Songs of Cherubs

Hark! the carol heavenward floats;
Listen to the liquid notes:
Listen well and you may hear
Songs of cherubs hovering near.

EUGENE FIELD

GOD REST YOU MERRY, GENTLEMEN

God rest you merry, gentlemen!

Let nothing you dismay,

For Jesus Christ, our Saviour,

Was born upon this day

To save us all from Satan's power

When we were gone astray:

O tidings of comfort and joy,

For Jesus Christ our Saviour

Was born on Christmas Day.

English Mincemeat Pie

INGREDIENTS

Mincemeat Filling

3 cups mincemeat (1 28-oz. jar)

1 cup chopped apple

½ cup chopped pear

¼ cup chopped walnuts or pecans

1 tablespoon finely grated orange zest

2 teaspoons finely grated lemon zest

¼ teaspoon freshly grated nutmeg

2 tablespoons butter

Pie Dough

2 cups all-purpose flour

1 teaspoon salt

6 tablespoons (¾ stick) chilled butter, cut up

6 tablespoons chilled vegetable shortening, cut up

5 to 6 tablespoons ice water

COOKING INSTRUCTIONS

Pie Dough

Mix the flour and salt and then add the butter and shortening. Use a knife or your fingertips to blend until the mixture resembles coarse crumbs.

- Sprinkle the ice water a tablespoon at a time over the flour mixture, tossing until the dough just comes together. Gather the dough into a ball, wrap it in plastic, and refrigerate it for at least 1 hour or for up to 2 days.

- Divide the dough into 2 pieces, one slightly larger than the other. Return the smaller piece to the refrigerator. On a lightly floured surface, roll the larger piece of dough into a 12-inch circle. Lay the circle into a 9-inch pie plate and trim any overhang.

Mincemeat Filling

Preheat oven to 400°F.

- Combine the mincemeat, apples, pears, nuts, and orange and lemon zest in a large bowl. Add the nutmeg and toss to combine. Spoon the filling into the pie crust, mounding it slightly in the center. Dot with butter, if desired.

- On a lightly floured surface, roll the smaller piece of dough into a 10-inch circle. Lay the circle on top of the mince-meat filling, crimping the edges together with a fork. Cut 2 or 3 air vents in the top crust.

- Bake for 30 to 35 minutes, until bubbling and lightly browned.

HARK! THE HERALD ANGELS SING

Hark! the herald angels sing,
"Glory to the new-born King;
Peace on earth, and mercy mild,
God and sinners reconciled!"
Joyful all ye nations rise,
Join the triumph of the skies;
With th' angelic host proclaim,
"Christ is born in Bethlehem."
Hark! the herald angels sing,
"Glory to the new-born King."

Hail, the heaven-born Prince of Peace!
Hail, the Sun of Righteousness!
Light and life to all He brings,
Risen with healing in His wings.
Mild He lays His glory by,
Born that man no more may die,
Born to raise the sons of earth,
Born to give them second birth.
Hark! the herald angels sing,
"Glory to the new-born King."

CHARLES WESLEY

WITH IVY
AND LAUREL,
AND BRIGHT
HOLLY BERRY,

BE CHRISTMAS
TO YOU
BOTH HAPPY
AND MERRY.

Merry Christmas with Love Merry Christmas with Love Merry Christ
Merry Christmas with Love Merry Christmas with
with Love Merry Christmas with Love Merry Christ
Merry Christmas with Love Merry Christmas with Lo
y Christmas with Love Merry Christmas with Love M
with Love Merry Christmas with Love Merry Christmas
Christmas with Love Merry Christmas with Love Merr
ve Merry Christmas with Love Merry Christmas with
y Christmas with Love Merry Christmas with Love M
s with Love Merry Christmas with Love Merry Chr
y Christmas with Love Merry Christmas with Love M
with Love Merry Christmas with Love Merry Christ
e Merry Christmas with Love Merry Christmas with
with Love Merry Christmas with Love Merry Christ
Merry Christmas with Love Merry Christmas with Lo
y Christmas with Love Merry Christmas with Love Lo
with Love Merry Christmas with Love Merry Christm
Christmas with Love Merry Christmas with Love Merr